# The Hand that Life Dealt Me

## McKenna Flint

BookLeaf Publishing

Presentation by *BookLeaf Publishing*

Web: www.bookleafpub.com

E-mail: info@bookleafpub.com

ISBN: 9789395621212

First edition 2022

# DEDICATION

To all those are suffering from a mental health disorder

And to all those that didn't make it through,

My prayers are with you always.

# ACKNOWLEDGEMENT

I want to thank everyone that never gave up on me.
My beautiful grandmothers, Bom and Granny, my dad, my Mama, every one of my amazing siblings, and of course, my two wonderful children and the man that made them possible.
I love you all unconditionally. Thank you for all of your support along the way.

And the biggest of thanks goes out to Halle Hovde for illustrating my cover. You can find more of her artwork at @handmadeby.Halle on Instagram.

# At the Ripe Age of Seven

At the ripe age of seven,
He made me a teacher.
From ABC's to 123's,
I taught him.

At the ripe age of seven,
A doctor I became.
Patching up scars and kissing away the pain,
Nurse is what I played.

At the ripe age of seven,
A mother is what you made me.
All so you could add to your family tree,
But a mother is something you'd never be.

You spread your legs
And I paid the price.
Instead of gaining a brother,
I became a mother.

Taking childhood games and making them my
harsh reality,
I became a pawn in a game I never asked to play,
At the ripe age of seven.

# Paddle

I was only nine when you first raised your hand
to me,
Only that hand was filled with a paddle.
And you expected me not to tattle,
But I was only nine when you first beat me.

I watched as you struck the ones I held most
dear,
My brothers, my best friends,
Your children in despair.

How could a mother do that to her children?

# Anxiety

A sense of vacuity consumes me.
I am engulfed in a harrowing feeling of being
sequestered and alone.
I must escape my head, the cage that binds me,
Or this anxiety that has taken root in me,
Will surely swallow me whole.

# The Day She Said Goodbye

I had been praying for this day for years,
But I never truly thought it would come.
To give up her own children,
That is something that a real mother could have
never done.

Don't worry about me, I was better off.
But how can you live with yourself
When you weren't there when we needed you
most?
How can you live without holding us close?
You were supposed to be the one that loved us
the most.

# Dear "Mother"

Like the whispers of the wind on a cold winter's
night,
Your voice echoes through my body,
Your conviction chills my soul.
Sometimes I am still gullible enough to believe
those words that you instilled in me,
Time and time again,
It's like they are plastered on my skin.

Well, Mother,
I am here today, and I will be here the next,
To continue to remind you
That despite what you made me believe,
I am more than good enough.

# A Home of Four Generations

The love ran deep,
Both in our bones and in our home.
We were blessed with a home of four
generations.
Always backed,
Support is something we never lacked.
No, our lives certainly weren't traditional,
But they were filled with true love,
Unconditional.

# Mama

You came into my life in the eighth grade
And to this day, you are the best friend that I've
made.
I think I got a fair trade
In the game of musical mothers.

Kissed away the pain
And even when you had nothing to gain,
You taught me how to battle the monsters.

Always there,
Like a breath of fresh air,
You became the one I could rely on.

Thank you for taking me in
And making me a part of your kin.

In saving me from my trauma,
You showed me what it means to be a mama.

# I'm Sorry I Destroyed You

You were everything and nothing, all at once
Everything
Because I saw the sun and the moon in your
eyes
And your love was enough to brighten the
darkest parts of me,
But also nothing,
Because the way I loved you was never built to
last
You were always destined to be a part of my past
And that surely wasn't by your design.
You were my knight in shining armor,
Defending me from the dragons that filled my
life.
But you should have been defending yourself
from me.
Armed with toxic traits and narcissistic ways
I inherited from my parents,
I was bound to be your downfall.
I'm sorry I destroyed you.

# Fighter

And though the essence of my soul runs cold,
I still hold on to my light.
For I will not let you drown out my light
Just to make your's shine brighter.
Grandma always told me I was a fighter.
That is the one thing I won't let you take from
me.
Because the rest of me
You already stripped bare.
Believing you cared,
I let you take everything I had
As you robbed me of my clothes, my innocence,
and my ability to say no.
Because the more times the word slipped from
my lips,
The more it lost it's conviction.

# Indelible Scars

And as the knife etched indelible scars into her
skin, little did she know
She would soon be etching those scars into the
heart of anyone who ever loved her.

She surrendered to the pain,
But she only caused them more.
Letting her blood succumb her body as she fell
to the floor,
This was the end of her story.

Let this be a lesson for it not to be yours.

# Psychiatric Hospital

I always denied, tried to pretend,
But as soon as that knife pierced my skin,
The illusion was over.

I was nowhere near fine,
But I was sure I didn't want to die,
Despite what my brain was telling me.

Chemical imbalances suffering in silence no
longer,
I fought to make myself stronger.

These walls may not have been the end of my
fight against my mind,
But they were the beginning of my fight to
survive.

# Bipolar Disorder

My brain drifts
As if it resonates with the sea,
In and out the waves crash.
They say that this is normal when you have
bipolar disorder,
But that does not take away the fear.
The sea is wild
And the gusts of wind are strong.
I can feel an episode coming on.
Soon, this sea will experience a hurricane
And I am scared of what destruction it will leave
in it's wake.

# Red Wine is Permanent

I let you spill yourself on to me,
Like I was the blank page of a journal
Just waiting to be filled.
You left stains on me,
Like red wine, rather than ink,
Intoxicating in the moment and soaked through
every page.
You varnished every part of me with a part of
yourself.
We were twin flames, one in the same,
Permanent imprints on each other.
Until you tried to strip away those beautiful
splashes
That left artwork across my pages.
You tried to soak up all of the wine
So you could imprint that same composition into
another journal
Before my pages had even dried off.

But, Silly Boy, didn't you know that red wine is
permanent?

There is still a blemish of you on each of my
pages

And I know there wasn't quite enough wine for
you to fill all of her folio,
Because you left some of it here on mine.

# Frail Frame

My frail frame collapses on the bed.
Not my bed, of course,
Because I can no longer sleep there,
 it is haunted with memories of you.
Tears drench the pillow case.
Not mine, of course,
Because everytime I lay my head to rest,
Images of you come flooding through.
Everywhere I turn, everywhere I look,
I'm reminded of the beautiful memories that you
have given me.
But the pain and sorrow that accompany them is
tearing me apart.
I am nothing but a frail frame,
An empty corpse.

# Addiction

Your love runs deep
As if a needle is in my sleeve,
You intoxicate me.
It is an addiction.
Only, for the first time in my life,
Addiction tastes sweet.
Sweeter than anything I have yet tasted
Or will ever taste.
This is not fiction,
Your love has become my solo addiction.
The only addiction that I would never dare fight
off.
Your love is my forever.

# Little Angel of Mine

Growing inside of me,
This seed of life,
Begging the best of me,
Guiding me to a better life.

Oh, how you have changed me
In, oh, so little time.
I promise to be my best for you,
Little angel of mine.

Mommy will be your guardian
And your teacher,
And you will be my pride.
You are Mama's everything already,
And you are still a part of me,
Growing deep inside.

# Granny

Sending me signs in the form of hummingbirds
and rainbows,
I know you are with me still
Reminding me of the morals you instilled.
My compass in life and in death,
You have always guided me.

# PTSD

Everything I had ever heard or read
Said that PTSD just wasn't for me,
Reserved for soldiers and the truly wounded.
If only I had realized that the wounded included
me.

It would have saved me a lot of drama and
heartache.
It would have made sense why my heart quaked
At the mere thought of getting close to someone.
I would have known why my own thoughts
Could make my heart beat through my throat
And ruin the brightest of days.
And it would have been crystal clear
Why the images that flooded my head
Left me wishing that I was dead.

So the doctors arranged a drug train
To rearrange the chemicals in my brain
And to stop the constant fluctuation of serotonin.

Now, I am nowhere near fine
But at least I can define
The monster that destroyed me.
Or was it one of the other nine
That followed closely behind,
I am an endless parade of lunacy.

# Two Walking Reminders

I have two walking reminders
That I am beyond blessed.
My God,
By my children I am utterly impressed.

I have two walking reminders
To always give my best,
Through anger and tears,
And every time that I'm put to the test.

I have two walking reminders
That my heart lives outside of my chest.

# Optimism

In order to survive,
My mind has trained itself
To be high, up in the sky.

Suspended between time zones and
atmospheres,
I get acquainted with the clouds.

It is safer up here,
No longer constricted.
Gravity and pain,
No longer one in the same.

I am free of my restraints,
Soaring high, up in the sky.
I can go anywhere from here.

# The Hand that Life Dealt Me

I let my breakdowns create breakthroughs
And used all of my pain to start anew.
And it was worth it,
For it got me here today.
This was the hand that life dealt me,
And so far, I've made it out okay.
I am a survivor
And I'm filled with an earnest desire
To always make it through.